Listen, Love

Listen, Love

Patricia Goedicke

Barnwood 1986

First printing
ISBN 0-935306-39-0
Library of Congress Catalog Card Number 85-72585

Grateful acknowledgement is made to the following magazines for first publication of poems in this book: *The American Poetry Review* for "All the Princes of Heaven" and "Hands That Have Waved Farewell," *Ascent* for "The Disappearance," *Back Door* for "Dust City," *The Chariton Review* for "Daily the Ocean between Us" (then published in the Doubleday *Anthology of American Poetry*) and "What the Maps Don't Mention, the Directions Never Say," *Choice* for "The World Pressing Itself Upon Us," *The Chowder Review* for "On the Tightrope" and "You Think I'm Your Worst Enemy," *Glassworks* for "The First Steps," *The Hampden-Sydney Review* for "Lucky" and "Though We Live Between Jaws," *Harvard Magazine* for "Something About Sticks," *Hearse* for "The Burning," *Hubbub* for "Chaplinesque (2)," *Iowa Review* for "My Mother's/My/Death/Birthday," (then published in *Psyche: The Feminine Poetic Consciousness*), *Ironwood* for "Moving/In One Place," *The Massachusetts Review* for "In the Hope of Whose Return," *The Missouri Review* for "The Arrival," *The Nation* for "The Athlete," "The First Forty Years Like a Puffball," "Moving With You," and "The Stars from Their Tall Posts," *New Letters* for "After the First Embrace" and "Crossing the Same River," *Open Places* for "The Sun Around Your Eyes" (then published in *The Sound of a Few Leaves*), *Perspective* for "Dear X," *Ploughshares* for "In the Middle of the Worst Sickness," *Poetry* for "The Core" and "Love Song: for the Four Corners," *Poetry Northwest* for "Green Harbor" and "This Man (Who Wants to Forget the Nightmare)," *Shenandoah Review* for "Two Weeks," *Three Rivers Poetry Journal* for "Over Our Dead Bodies" and "Rose," *Three Sisters* for "In This Fog," *Waves* for "Like Animals," and *Wind* for "Her Answer" and "Letter to King Love."

Author's Note:
In addition to their appearance in magazines, many of these poems, though by no means all of them, have also, though in rather random fashion, appeared in previous volumes of the author's work. This present collection, however, is confined entirely to the love poems, and is intended to be read as a deliberate sequence.
The author would like to take this occasion to thank all of those involved in the publication of her earlier books of poetry, as well as, for this present one, most especially her friend and editor Tom Koontz and, as always, her husband.

Photograph of Patricia Goedicke and Leonard Robinson by Miki Boni.
Graphics by Barbara LaRue King.

The Barnwood Press
Rt 2 Box 11C
Daleville, IN 47334

Printed in The United States of America.

For Leonard

Contents

IV THE BURNING

V MOVING/IN ONE PLACE

VI THOUGH WE LIVE BETWEEN JAWS

"Love is not a condition; it is a direction."
—Simone Weil

Love Song: for the Four Corners

Keeper of the doorknob.
Keeper of the latchstring.
Keeper of the sword within.

Lakes.
Twins.
Together on the mountain:
Rider
Root
Peg.
Tongue obscured
Where earth meets sky

Horseman, flower.
Corncob.
Egg.
Joiner.

I.   The Sun Around Your Eyes

My Mother's/My/Death/Birthday

Now almost everything I ever imagined
Has caught up with me:
The death defying leap that worked,
The desert years that flowered,
Now the shadow has found a bed to lie down in,
I have come back from the cemetery of divorce:
Having sucked strength
From her tears, turned
Her denial into second growth
Now in my 39th year as if it were the 9th month
Heavy with summer, filled
To overflowing by the good man
She always meant me to marry,
I see him standing like an orchard
Over all the dry days of her dying:
Though the ache of her absence is the first bruise
On the blossoming plum she bore
Now even as the world descends
My mother my mold my maker
Is with me to the end:
Now the hand in the glove of the body,
The soul moves freely and well,
Pockets rolling with the stars of the one man
I always meant to love and now can.

Lucky

(On June 21, 1976)

By sheer accident having met him,
The man with harvest in his pockets,

With clean new irrigation ditches
And oranges and other fruit trees,

With harrow and fertilizer and honey
And pickaxes and pepper in his eyes

Outside the house I had locked
And barricaded against flood

The land all around it is mine
And rises up to me

Gently, on either side of the river
He has returned it to me

With a sense of balance,
With water under my arms like wings

And even though I capsize often,
Though rocks rake my cheeks,

Though fear rides the center current,
The shape of it shadowy, defined

By dim flashings, foghorns,
The noose tightening around my neck,

Though the life that pretends to float me
Is honeycombed with emptiness, great pits

The first hollowings of the disease
That is sucking everyone's strength away

Because he says so it is easy
Simply to go right on bailing,

Patching up the leaks but hardly noticing,
Sailing along with the wind

Power comes to the right hand
Skill tingles in the left

Relishing even the dangerous rapids
Everything seems brand new

And beautiful, even after forty-five years
All the doors of the house are wide open,
And the river running through it.

Green Harbor

I waited for you on the beach
Where the ocean liners passed by

Over the horizon and left me
Their cruel smokestacks.

Foam shuffled at my feet,

Impatient sandpipers skittered
Back and forth in their neat wedges

52 playing cards all turned
One way

I thought no one would ever meet me
Climb my solitary tower

I thought I would be cast away
On an empty coconut shell bobbing

Then you came riding
The one rail of morning

You whispered in my ear
My dear

Where you are going I'm coming
With you don't worry

Don't think of them the liners
Pass by and carry us with them

Foam-flowers in their wake

You know I would never leave you:
Now I have leapt the sun

My body is a rope of rubies
Fish heading straight for shore

Now the grotto is filled
Almost to the top

It is a clear pail
Of silver champagne we swim

Two seahorses suspended

Now I am a fan of light
A girl combing her hair

In the green falling a tree
Trembles in the wind, a harp

Bent to its knees and moaning
Down to its ankles my braids undone

Curl over the waist of the waves

Now as you fold me
Now as you spread me out

Hearts and diamonds in whole necklaces

The single note of a loon
Wails me down the stone steps

To where you are waiting, to a world
I drown in and then rise

With open fists palm upwards
To your face now mine;

In a charm of emeralds drifting
Back and forth in the harbor

For a little while it is certain the sea
All around us means no harm, no harm.

The Sun Around Your Eyes

Out in the back garden
Wild roses break
Over the curls of your hair

Your muscular arm
In a thick sweater lifts

The dog, shining
Black, in a red collar

Into the air around
The sun around your eyes
Yellow nasturtiums flutter

All over the dazed
Blue mountain morning

Between red tongues
White butterflies bubble

Mexican pointsettias
Star the green trees.

Two Weeks

Whenever you have to leave me
It is as if all the days had given away their names
And all my thoughts with them.

Flying around these two weeks
Lazy as paper airplanes

Hovering over beds, tables, chairs
They slip out of the windows so fast
It is almost impossible to catch them,

The hours flow together like silk
Peacefully, beneath my feet

Each length of sunshine is watermarked
With your initials and mine

As if we were really twins
The paint is applied so smoothly there's no telling
Where one stroke begins or the other ends

But especially now, with you gone
Everything is almost too much,
No matter how beautiful the blank white sheets

Without you to stub my toe on,
Without you bellowing at me from the bedroom

I'm weightless, anonymous as a ghost
Drifting uneasily through the house

Always there is this puzzlement in my blood,
All day there is this dim ache, this hollowness
As if some part of me had gone to sleep.

In This Fog

It is as if the wing of an ant
Had whisked away the world.

Ashen, weightless,
Even the lovers, offstage

Are hushed, speechless,
Whispering to each other the way the trees

Shell them in shadow like fans,
Like fringed fingers caress,

Weave them into a breathing frieze
Until they become all air, air

And lighter than air they move
With winged tentative feet

Onto the stage at last,
As the footlights finally begin to flare

Without knowing it they begin to chatter
And stumble, forgetting their lines until

With blurred faces, like rowboats in gray,
With a soft shock they bump

Belly to belly like June bugs they fall
Into each other, into the blaze of day.

The First Forty Years Like a Puffball

But this morning I'm lying here in bed
Breathing easy.

Plump pincushion with no pins in it
Relaxed, dusty
Puffball sitting on an old bureau

And the years, yes, the years
Of course will stick more pins in me
As they go by

Still there is no taste like the taste of the clouds
Swirling around this mountain,

Bald hilltop stuck all over with pinetrees
But beautiful, I say, over the red earth
Swinging my arms at the sky

And looking down from the heights of my head
· Over the lumps of my body remark
As yet there are few damages to assess

And would have been less
If I had brought you this small piece of ground,
This green hummock for you to stand on
If I had brought myself to you sooner —

Then what?
My first forty years like a stuck pig,

Like a wounded porcupine bristling
Inside my own fence, my steel cage
I had to spend climbing

To reach you.

But now, on this summit,
The thick branches of your arms
Sheltering my nakedness like a fur coat

At long last I am able to look out
And down
Like anyone else the world stretches before me

Behind clouds bleeding, mysterious
But still beautiful, and with a degree of calm.

Hands That Have Waved Farewell

Hands that have waved farewell
Meaning, we still meet again,

Cities I had thought lost forever
That have returned to me,

Sooner or later I will see them again, the mountains
The white coffee cup beside my plate

Steaming in the cold, as suddenly solid
As the most miraculous happening

In the whole world, it is a gift
That is given to everyone, yes

Everyone:
The patterns of our lives

Repeat themselves, like the old woman
Who keeps looking into your eyes from a window

Right next to the tracks as the train passes
On its way to forgotten farmhouses,

The strict pine trees of New Hampshire
Like night watchmen in the snow. . . .

For me it was a small town in Mexico
Flamboyant, full of flowers

Lying on a hillside with the moon
And bittersweet stars in its hair

But for me also it was the one man
I did not recognize,

At every turning point in my life
Like a small pony he would be standing there

Like an armchair with a cello in it, or a brook
He kept beckoning to me like the sun

Or a coffee cup, full of warmth
Until I accepted him, so that now

In the thick snows of New Hampshire,
In the dry deserts of Mexico

Over and over I keep finding them
Rustling in the wind like leaves,

Like growth rings in the book of trees
Hands that have waved farewell,

Cities I had thought lost forever
That have returned to me.

II. This Man

The Arrival

Luggage first, the lining of his suit jacket dangling
As always, just when you'd given up hope
Nimbly he backs out of the taxi

Eyes nervously extending, like brave crabs
Everywhere at once, keeping track of his papers
He pilots himself into the home berth

Like a small tug in a cloud of seagulls
Worries flutter around him so thick
It takes him some time to arrive

And you wonder if he's ever really been happy:
When the blue eyes blur
And stare out to sea

Whether it's only a daydream
Or a long pain that silences him
In such gray distances

You'll never know, but now
Turning to you, the delicate mouth
Like a magician

Is curious, sensitive, playing tricks,
Pouting like a wise turtle
It seems he has a secret

With the driver,
With the stewardess on the airplane
So that even when he opens his arms,

When the warm voice surrounds you,
Wraps you in rough bliss,
Just before you go under

Suddenly you remember:
The beloved does not come
From nowhere: out of himself, alone

Often he comes slowly, carefully
After a long taxi ride
Past many beautiful men and women

And many dead bodies,
Mysterious and important companions.

The First Steps

He begins simply, like a skater,
He imitates a skater.

Sitting on a hard chair
This plump gray haired man
With both legs dangling

Speaking of thin ice he takes off,
One foot sashays
Swiftly after the other,

Circling and swooping he glides
Without moving from his place.

Everyone around him is all Business,

But over the polished floor
Frozen surfaces begin to heave.

Next time he gives himself up
To the elegant body of a bird.

Among the Serious Observers
Motionless, crouched behind their blinds,

Suddenly he's smiling,
Hopping on one foot

The pudgy arms flap,
The feathers of his hair whiten,

To everyone's astonishment

Suddenly we know what it feels like
To be a bird!

Next he's telling us how men
First came to believe in gods:

Talking out loud to the sky,
Those cloud deities piled up there,
Reclining on blue air,

All at once he's one of them;

The round chest billows out,
The crumpled profile rears up
Majestic, over our heads

And whether he intends to or not
He appeals to each of us,

One after the other, tentatively

We take our first cautious steps
On the ice.

The Athlete

And sometimes, when the sun stands up
Right out of the ground

There's no doubt about it,
You're talking to a young man.

Sudden as a haystack or a geyser
Spouting a hatful of gold coins

Some kind of supernatural
Athletic energy fills the air

And you fall back
In astonishment, O
Where is misery, irony, despair?

Brassy, wearing the blue sky
Perched on his head like a bowler

He smiles like James Cagney playing George M. Cohan
Until you can't help staring:

Houses jump for joy,
Trees shine, and the birds with them,
Something takes your breath away

Those rare days when he winks
As if it were all true,
As if there were some hope

After him even old hearts
Bounce in their beds like children,

Like a heavenly beachball he rolls on
Right through town like a trumpet.

The Last Man

On the day the last man
Came to the edge of the land

Salt stuck to his hair
Streaming straight behind him

The cold sea rose
Over his domed head

But he like a lion thinking,
That day with his bulk

His curl, his small
Tough heart he made

The whole shoreline gather
Around his stubborn profile,

The wind swallowed his words
And the waves his clumsy feet

But still in his fur cap
And green bulge of coat

He strode the sand, foolish
But grand.

Rose

May not be tough enough for most men but he
Is many throated, rich, with lights

Carving beautiful red palaces

Wherever he is, in flannels
Or dungarees, picking himself up

Strong as the footsteps of a mountain

Inside the honeycombed globe of his head
Whole landscapes appear like magic,

The pieces of his life open out

On the pillow next to me there's a garden
Full of excitement, the hum

Of a hundred live birds

That soar like arrows or chirp
Sassy as sparrows in the dust,

Red-breasted, flashing back and forth

Out of the intricate depths,
The complicated corridors of his body

The idea of fire emerges,
Scarlet petal upon petal,

Fold upon fold of it like an overcoat,
Like a deep red heart beating

Secretly, in and out,

For if there are worms within he conceals them,
As a proud emblem he appears

Carnation colored, triumphant
Blazoned on a dark ground

For his anger cuts like a sword
In all directions laying waste

But swifter than lightning, as soon over
For the sake of everyone around him,

For the sake of the children next door

The delicate leaves of his lips curve,
Smiling their wise, archaic smile

For his courage is a beehive
Many-chambered, full of fragrance

To protect the innocent in velvet,

In the odor of summer flourishing
Like scented linen, like honey

His gaiety pours over everything,
Like a small satyr, on his toes

As clumsy as he is graceful,
Pirouetting on the lawn

Fearlessly, flexing his muscles
His fingers are a network

Stretching far and near

The heat of his hand is like warm earth
That has been soaking in the sun for years.

On the Tightrope

Back and forth between all those needy friends,
Beloved family, dinnerguests, houseguests

With time slipping away like food
Cooked, eaten, badly digested

She thinks she will die of too much vacation

But she has forgotten him
And what a juggler he is:

Even in this strange town
He keeps them all in orbit,

Bouncing on the one hand beds for everyone,
On the other a place for her

He brings it right along with them,

The sun like a dog on a string,
A warm spot, a piece of privacy

There, in the quiet study
Among the shallow breathing

Of the poems she writes, those thin tightropes
She keeps trying to sing

Even though it's he, really,
He at the front door balancing

Plates, glasses, people like tired planets,
He takes care of everything.

Chaplinesque (2)

Gestures made against snow:
The fling

And scatter of birdseed onto burned grass.

At every feeding station the arch
Of each age is ridiculous to the next.

The trajectory of a slingshot.

Man hurls his aircraft into the night sky:
Frail scarves, rhinestones

Wink against the stars

While you tiptoe on the ice, neat bottomed,
Stringy against cold bushes.

With one eye on your audience you advance
As if you were on stage, absurd

But perfect, teetering on one foot, mocking
A ballet dancer busy at his grace.

Birds dash themselves across the landscape

But out there at the feeder like a football player
Flipping your small hands

Old man you are my old man:
Every play you make is a grandstand.

Moving With You

is like flying
but then everything is like flying
with you: moving
or standing still,

right now
wheeling like a crazy pony
up here on the roof
of your new apartment building

on top of all the people
lumped, laddered below us
you're wearing your clown's suit,
you're so deliciously funny
and so moving

you say any horse
worth his humanity
of course knows what it feels like
to be thrown out, dragged after —

entertaining us at a party
when you do the spastic
walk like a cripple,

fake loose leg,
dislocated jerk,
head and face lifted
above it all, it's obvious

every move Pegasus makes
with you holding the reins
you're flying, we're all flying
so high we don't notice the pain.

This Man
(Who Wants to Forget the Nightmare)

This man who can blow smoke rings like a kite
Swooping over the bed, who is two pillows

Or four or five, or a field of poppies, or ten fingers,
Chinese firecrackers in the morning,

This man who is the two halves of a walnut
Opening out into a waterfall

This man who is pure muscle, a silk shirt
Rippling like the Aurora Borealis

This man who expands
From pleasure to pleasure like laughing gas

This man will confess anything,
Comforting businessmen, and drunks

With his arms around lonely women
This man who is spontaneous

Hotblooded, eager to do battle
This man who is a lift home

On a rainy day, a clap on the back, a big handkerchief
In time

Because what he wants most is to forget the nightmare
Of everyone's growing up

This man who was mugged once
Listening to other people's problems

On streetcorners, helping out beggars
Promising what he can't deliver

This man who wants to be a hero,
A brave regiment, a banner

This man is a geranium,
Blooming like happiness on the kitchen sink,

This man is a wool overcoat
For wrapping up pain, for putting it to sleep

This man who is wide open, deep chested, a trunk
Overflowing with old costumes, successful ideas, mistakes

This man who is bottomless, a still pond
Under a gray sky

This man will offer everything he has to everyone
Who passes by.

III.   What the Maps Don't Mention

In the Living Room

There's an elephant in the kitchen!
Huge friendly bulk,

Four flatiron feet on the floorboards,
Domed back humping the ceiling . . .

In the living room the piano sways,
Lifts itself up on tiptoe

Out in the hallway the stairs stretch
Almost as far as the stars

The front porch hums like a harp
The chimney breathes a long sigh
Of relief

In the bedroom where it all began
The cellar sinks
Deeper

Lion tamers and ballerinas
And dwarf butter babies flood the whole house

As she takes off her hat to him,
He lifts his to her.

The Core

Blackbird, burrowing
Into my deepest cave

You fly straight in
Strong as a snake

In your arms
Strange, strange

Everything forgets,
Everything falls away

Even the glow from the street
Finally goes out

In these black veins
All the animals in the world

In slow motion gather,
Jostling each other with their soft sighs

Turtle next to bird,
Dim tiger, lamb

Kangaroo, mouse, mole
But here there are no questions,

Here everyone is blind
Hunting the seeds of light

And we among them, dumb
As two coal miners digging

Underneath everything for the core
Only darkness ignites.

The Disappearance

The two people on the bed
Have just cut themselves out of the picture.

Blackness pours over them like syrup, where is
His knee or her thigh

Hands wetly dissolved in
Soft boxing gloves with

No inner outlines anywhere,
There is a black cave

In the middle of the world shaped
Like one silhouette of two

Oval bodies beauti-
Fully folded in each other, the twin

Blades of a pair of scissors shut
In thick plush muffled

All around them the white sheets
Of the outside world disappear,

Naked in the bottomless lake
Under the typewriter's dustcover

Keys jam, paintbrushes marvelously run
Into each other, smoothly the animal

Bones move loosely inside the blind
Plump skin relaxed now almost

With no mind, no definition at all
Piece by piece division

Stops fighting, gives up, goes to sleep
To the low blurred humming

Of two plants opening
Out into their insides

Ebony drips like a heavy faucet
Down through the mattress sinking

Into one of the many secret
Black pockets of the universe

Among the thousands curled up,
Furled around themselves

There where children nestle
Soundlessly exploding but safe

Powerfully they suck at everything,
Deep in the ooze, reborn

Into this last luxury
As toes, fingers, private

Now vanishing parts fuse
Into black asterisks, mysterious
As the other side of stars. . . .

What the Maps Don't Mention, the Directions Never Say

Who knows where we're going?
I am thinking, perhaps
That you are thinking
Maybe . . .

Today, in the air
There was a hint,
The quiver of your
Glance

Therefore I brush my teeth,
Clean my breath
For you only but say nothing.

Of course I would like to speak,
But who knows where we're going?

Rain
Walks across the roof.

Like two peaches,
Two plums
Wrapped in a cockleshell bed

I read,
You read
As usual but underneath
Something is tugging at the boat.

Words in the shy corners
Of both our mouths wait,
Wait to be shown the way . . .

Then, in the darkness, crisp
And brisk as winter, our clean
Fragrant pajamas slide
Somewhere out of sight,

But who could have known
Before, you

Like a bright ski-jumper
Yellow as the sun would leap
Into my arms like water, like snow, like ice

Stiff as feathers our words would drop
With every other intelligence
Flashing like scales from our eyes,

The flowers of the rain would open,
Like two jubilant seagulls we would fly

Far out over the diamond,
The trackless circle of the ocean.

All the Princes of Heaven

First it is only the sense of sunlight
Creeping up over the dunes

Darkness is beginning to pale
Imperceptible sounds

In every corner of the house there are shiftings
Minute, barely distinguishable

The delicate slow tide rises
Out on the long marshes

Something is running through the tall grass
Crinkling it with excitement

Inside it is as if they were moving furniture
The heavy velvet of the couch
Blunders over to the window

The crisp curtains are beginning to breathe
Fronds of your hair sweep
Back and forth along the floor

Out on the porch of your thighs
Sandpipers flicker, with their little feet

From one fiber to the next
The flat wooden planks are beginning to swell

Now the seagulls are impatient, mewing
And flapping their wide wings,

Turning your quiet abdomen into a loud
Fourth of July Day crowd

With flags waving, people
Jostling each other on the street

Your breasts are beginning to ache,
They are turning into Scylla and Charybdis

But softer, with hearts of butter,
Nipples of pure cream

Your teeth open and close like the jaws
Of a ravenous whale but gentle,
Rolling in its own sweet wake

The inner and outer lips are turning purple
Stretching themselves like a child sucking

The agitated motion of the round pilings
On either side of the dock increases

Waves slap back and forth
Both buttocks are jerking

The white galaxies of night
Inhabit the day, in a trance

The orange prow of the ship appears
Over the horizon it shoves its way
Across the smooth sheets

Shooting stars and colored streamers
And twenty-one gun salutes

All the princes of heaven come
Leaping onto the land,

Exploding together into dawn
The earth shakes itself to pieces,

In the hot arms of the sun
The sides of the waiting wharf heave
Up to the sky and then down.

Like Animals

Over her like a dog
Muscular, tricky, neat

And she under, oh under
Nuzzling the nipple of the prick,
The shaggy brush of the balls

In the depths of summer
In the heat
In the red shadows of the bedroom

His belly like the ceiling
Arms and legs like doorposts

And she brown as the floorboards
Beneath him, jiggling like a pup

In the muddle of their bodies
Grappling for each other's souls

They are feeding on each other so fiercely
They are barely able to speak:

Locked in the cave of the self
They are all alone, they are lonely

Loneliness spreads like a hole in their chests
Wheezing for breath, in darkness

Like a bone stuck in a beast's craw
In the kitchen it is a brown shadow,
A whiff of sad air....

Nevertheless, between them
Every once in awhile there is a quick flashing,
A sort of gurgling song:

With the bloated golden guts
Of turtle, snake, swan

With fine, spirited fingers
And nimble, intelligent feet

In a whirr of mischievous wings
They cling to each other like animals

And oh it is sweet, it is sweet.

The Melting

You breathing like a brook,
Your sleep flowing away

Fists the air of the earth
Back with a yawn.

Lumped in the hollows of the bear
With shoulders and back that tell
The long yarns of winter,

By the sack of the body dinted
Down by the casseroles of the buttocks,
In the round scoops of the knees

Thick pools of scent
Gather on fur and blanket
Till the darkness is all flowers,

Snowfields pocked with stars,
Daisies matted in the ears
Of those great hairy beasts

Whose frozen presence first announced,
Then melted away but left
Their warm impressions on nothingness,

Spooned bowls of summer on ice.

Three Things

First thing this morning: your eyes
Like two violets on the pillow
Smiling:

Your cock curled up
In sleep but now stirring.

Second thing this morning:
The way we keep on going.

After a long night's
Iron attempt to forget

For a few hours at least
Almost the fear is over:

After a last armful of each other
Like two straws in the death wind

A donkey brays, the tin
And mournful churchbell clucks its tongue

Downstairs the maid comes in
On a cloud of Mexican orange juice

The smell of breakfast rises
And so do we; and so do we:
Third thing this morning.

IV. The Burning

Letter to King Love

Listen, Love,
Last night after trying
Unsuccessfully to convince yourself,
Next you tried to convince me,
Love, that you're neither King nor Thor
Nor Zeus nor even Poseidon;
Furthermore, when tired
Imagine yourself Achilles
(All men wounded, all men
Urgently desiring to crawl off
Into a corner and sulk)

Still, when you're King, Love,
Maker of new men, head of all joy
And heart, too,
Over and over and over
Friend, comforter, sustainer,
Who'd want to go on forever?

So you try to trick
The whole court to agree with you, if kings
Can't leave themselves the court certainly can,
Could be kicked out, you could
But only if you forget the glory,
Sun in the camp,
Meadows in the sky
And that thin string, the queen
At your side who'd wait
Forever for you to come back, knowing
The danger of it.

The Burning

This conversation is a conflagration.

Clanging like thirteen firebells you talk
Like a rain of metals, like dumbbells
Banging like brass in my ears.

So, I think I will turn myself into wet wood.
I think I will burn myself up.

Ah, what a smoke would be there.

I think you would choke
I hope

But no.

"Listen to me" you shout:
"It is because I love you
Most, like flame, in full bloom—"
I know, I know.

Sending up smoke signals from my past
I'm trying to prove it.

Once I thought men were woodcarvers,
I thought women should wrap themselves in cotton
And then go suffocate

But you won't do it,
Thank God here you come

Like a five alarm fire around the corner
With no water hose, nothing

You light me, you turn me
Into a clear tongue of fire

I love/my love/ together
First you burn, then I.

When You're Sick

When you're sick and can't talk to me
Oh what an occasion for despair!

The table gives me the hard edge of its hand,
The doorsill trips me up,

The bedroom turns into a child's playpen
With absolutely nothing in it

But you, of course, you
Lying there in a far corner, in my eyes

Shriveled into yourself, and so much like a dwarf
I can hardly see you...

Well, it is clear, then,
Nobody loves me
Or ever will again.

Banging my baby spoon on your head
I keep yelling at you to wake up, wake up

They're hurting me! Listen
Knowing you've been sick this long time
Why doesn't anyone pity *me*?

Instead everyone hates me,
You certainly won't lift a finger to help me

And how can I blame you?
Giving myself up to pure grief

I've turned our big bed into a cradle:
In the deserted doll house of my dreams

I'm ravelling around like a stuffed animal
Weeping cotton at the seams.

She Says His Pain Is Hers

The husband in his illness groans,
Paces the floor above.

The hairs of her head rise up
Waving like hungry sea anemones

But she does not dare go near him
Nor will she let him be.

When will he be well?
Or what is love

That sickens when it finds sickness?

Back and forth her soul sways
Swooning on the heels of his.

All night the salt
Tears fall like bright gouts of blood —

She says his pain is hers,
She cannot bear to speak.

Darling, she whispers up to him,
This suffering is murder.

Daily the Ocean Between Us
(Psalm for My 43rd)

After the first shallows have dropped out,
Leaving us gasping for breath

Suddenly the air is much thicker.
I swim in it, almost choking

Except for you

It is as if we had fallen into a blood pudding.

Wave upon wave of it rises,
Slowly the hot heaviness settles...

After 43 years I'm still struggling to get through
These sodden labyrinths that have sprung up

Everywhere around me:
Roots, water snakes, lilies...

Surely it is a kind of pleasure, this pain.

In the tender suck of the bayou
Mangroves caress our knees

But also there is this slow,
Powerful, deep pull:

In between rages, red-faced
Here we are, holding hands

Under water there is this current
Flowing like lava between us:

Teaching each other how to breathe
Gradually we move out to the center:

Wrestling together in the dark
Devouring chambers of the sea

At least, for awhile, we don't drown,
We fight side by side,

Each of us embraces the other
With fists or kisses, no matter:

Whenever you shift, I shift
From one stroke to the other,

Daily the ocean between us
Grows deeper but not wider.

You Think I'm Your Worst Enemy

You think I'm your worst enemy and perhaps I am,
    Most irritating because best loved, most intimate,
In the fogged blue hours of morning of course you blame me,
    Kick off the covers, god damn dependency, the helplessness of age

Which is what I can't stand either:
    I want to be the lightning rod
        That strikes back at the foul sky *for* you,
But you want to do it yourself: therefore I hide
    Under the leafmold of days I crouch

Beside your path, in every footstep twinned,
    Multiplying under thick mulch, near to you as mushrooms,
Close grizzled, prickly as the gray stubble
    Along your jaw line, the word on the tip of your tongue

You can't find, you have to ask me for help
    Which makes you furious, naturally, and then me too,
Almost crazed with it, the trivia, the constant forgetting
    But still I hunker down, knowing the magician will return

Any minute now, I wait for the grand dazzle,
    In the promise of warmth renewed
Maybe I curl myself around you like an old bedsock:
    The moss of my breathing clings to you, it will

Not let go, leeched to your soggy lungs
    I gasp for air, accuse you of taking it all
And then subside,
    In the brittle wheeze of the nostrils
        Though the bridge pinches, inside it is the thin saddle,

The breath that supports both of us, even though your wrists stiffen
    And rasp in their sockets like dry doorknobs,
Though the wobbly kite string of your pulse weakens,
    Feebly threads itself between us,

I tie myself to it, tightening the ring finger
    That binds both of us; you think I'm your angriest extremity
But really I'm ingrown, a sore toenail
    With no skin but yours, without you who would I be?

Maybe we get all tangled up in each other but how
  Can one end of the drawstring exist without the other?
I'm not your numb pigskin only,
    In the real scrimmage neither of us kicks the other around;
      Out on the hard highway maybe I'm the one pebble in your shoe

That won't go away; without it who would we be
  But dull, wooden as dead trees
And we know it, each day breaks out
    New leaves from old bark, strained muscles creak
      And snap at each other but keep on growing.

In the Hope of Whose Return

1

Caught in the family Volkswagen with you
Raging at me as you drive,

Myself retaliating, sometimes even
Initiating, the seats are so close together

Our luggage, packed in back
Keeps looming at us,

Telling us to shut up

Also the traveling kitchen, the first-aid kit
For emergency use only...

But this is an emergency!

Neither of us can get out
Even though the windows are wide open,

With air hurtling through them
Like a hurricane in a cage,

Even though our words
Tear at each other like fighting birds

In such tornadoes of misery
I'm flooding the armrest, swearing
Clawing at my own skin

While you like an angry blue jay
Tyrannical, in dizzy circles

Keep frightening me with pronouncements
Over and over of ruin, calamity,

You're leaving me tomorrow.....

2

So in the cycles of such wars
The car almost leaves the road

But doesn't, for cooped up here together
This intimacy is our own choice

Boiling and sputtering down the highway
In whatever fury with each other, yes,

We'd rather be here than out there,

Sliding along in a huge station wagon
So silently, and swift

Smug, self-satisfied, indifferent
With perfect dispositions, controlled

We'd turn into heroes and heroines
Larger than life, and shinier

Carefully streamlined and polished
But desperately dreaming, in our separate seats

Of green eyes flashing, eyes
Glittering at us from the far ends of the world

For here, at least, we remember,
(How close we are, how close)

Incestuous as twins, symbiotic
Locked in our steel womb

Strapped down by seat belts
Eating into our flesh,

By tongues like razors, like knives
Cutting each other's guts out

And then *explaining* them to each other
As if this were some sort of anatomy lesson,

This marriage is a live cadaver,
Like Plato's egg, seems doomed to separate

3

But will not, listen, but *will not*:

For as much as we choose anything, choose
Seeming self-destruction, choose

To lose ourselves in the familiar,
The chafing arms of each other

Surely the responsibility is ours

For every part of it,
The whole confused body
Of the cross we make together,

From side to center to side

Our wild outstretched wings
May hurl themselves in and out

As far from peace as they can get

But this agony, this torment
Is ours also, remember

Just as surely as we once chose

And keep on choosing it, the mothering
And all fathering eye of the storm

Where we first met, and embraced
Like doves balancing in air,
In the risky middle of our lives

Where the white feathers of our fingers
Clasp each other in a cathedral
Electric, full of the joyful calm

That began everything,
In the hope of whose sure return

So suddenly peaceful
And so unexpectedly gay

We keep together forever, no matter
How often we are swept away.

V.   Moving/In One Place

Waking at Night

Waking up beside you, for no reason
    Silent as water, in the middle of the night

Is it the slow moonrise
    Up through the toes to the stomach,
        The beautiful bell sounds of nothingness?

Floating
    On the thin bed like a ship
        Now dreams disappear,

The moon like a giant lemon
    The town in my mouth like an orange

The cobblestone streets of the bones, the river
    Blood-red in the starshine

The rocky eyebrows,
    The clear dust of the hair

The highways of my arms stretched out
    Across the desert to you

My nextdoor neighbor, my twin village
    Drifting on the lake of night

The pale steeples of the soul
    Subsided now, and quiet
        Bodies like bright leaves cut loose.

Where We Are

And what we say,
the sound of it, echoing
inhabits the hollow house
with the little ghosts of kisses,
what we leave behind us

but where we are no shadows.

The whole whispering world
fattens on them like a child
eating invisible honey

but where we are no noise,

only a high cloud sailing
on the pale hands of our tongues
white as towers, veiled, airy
up the stairs to the attic passing
even the immortal bed, which may fade
one deaf day may fold its sheets

but not tonight
but not tonight
moth wing, flying Dutchman

swallower of moonlight.

The Hook

Teetering on the lip of the present,

casting about, casting —
sunbather in daisies,
swimmer in white water
who would abandon the field of light

to write about it?

My life's too sweet to leave;
I'd lie here forever except

back upstream about a mile
once there was a miracle.

Nearer there's you,
your water lily face,
eyes rooted in rock pools,
rainbows pouring waterfalls —

Pierced by the hook of now
my life's too sweet to forget
one minute,

great trout or bluefish
shiny with meaning
against the rush of the rapids

let me drag it out.

The Stars from Their Tall Posts

Each night the bedroom turns into a cave
At the foot of a giant waterfall.

Even in our sleep we can hear it
Pouring water like the wind

Past the wide-open mouth of the cave
To great sheets of moonlight,
The black rock at the entrance

In pure silver drenched,
Quivering, cold, soaring...

All night long we keep swimming
In and out of our dreams.

Outside our windows the stars
Are talking to each other, in low voices

But we are too busy to listen,
As if we were children at play

You are a large cloud
Lying beside me, every once in awhile
Pricked by faint sparks of lightning

While I climb aloft, in the rigging
Strong as a seagull I grow wings...

Waking, I hear you snoring,
Huddled beside me as usual

But sleeping once more, on the dazzled ocean of the bed
Do I ask for you? Do you dream
For one moment of me?

As if the room were a boat,
As if we were blind sailors
Now everything disappears,

Adrift on a sea of miracles
The buoys that mark our passage,
The fires that shoot across the water

Now everything is cut loose
Wherever we go we will forget
Most of it by morning

But here, on the lap of night
It is impossible to go too far
Or too much alone:

The waterfall world rushes on
But the stars from their tall posts are watching,

In the dark cave of the bedroom, somehow
Something returns us to the harbor
Safely, just before dawn.

Moving/In One Place

What they are whispering, the two goldfish
Suddenly I know is your name.

Pressing their mouths against the glass
Their arms like two shreds of silk,
Orange silk, rippling

Are moving / moving / moving
Only to stay in one place,

The two honey colored bodies,
The tawny transparent tails...

In the yellow bell of a streetlight
The spiny petals of the snow fall.

Swept by the fins of night
Everything in the world undulates,

Shimmering,
Magnified by containment

Huge wings
Quivering
Against the glass sides of the bowl,

The golden valves of the soul.

Her Answer

O lamb
With the voice of a lion you lie down
Beside the turning globe.
The kingdoms of earth are yours,
And the kingdoms of all waters.
Enchanted skyscrapers topple,
All roads to Venice,
Chicago, Paris, Hong Kong
The mysterious town of Rindge
New Hampshire, superhighways
Sleepy rivers, subways
Turn on their heels and follow you

O lion
With the loud voice of a lamb
You roar in the treetops,
With the tongue
Of a wily milk snake suck
Till all peoples are yours,
Wisely you walk among them,
With your smooth face cajole,
Cozen them with your innocence,
With your fierce wit chastise
Encourage, raise them up

O lamb
With the lovely voice of a lion
Till all aching oceans, nerves,
Bones of sorrow subside
And curl around your feet, your smile
Dries up Noah's tears
At the bleat of your smallest anger
And the wrath of your brookless pity
The lion hums a love song
To the newborn one who roars
Softly softly softly
Through the whole world, I am
Yours.

Crossing the Same River

For the Continuity Man splices
Scene / after scene
Together

And then throws them away / helpless
Because they keep changing

They refuse to stay the same

They will gather no moss
He insists

Nobody ever took photographs of us
As children

We have changed,
Changed entirely from the time

In the quick burst
Of a flashbulb

Someone once said
Hold still / darling
Hold still . . . .

But I will remember
And you will remember

What we said before:

No bigger than a moth's shadow
With soft shaky wings

Something in us
Persists:

From one decade
To the next / registering

However delicately / pictures
That become part of us

What each of us is
And will be

Layers of living
Accumulate

Breath after breath / no heavier
Than marsh lights

Though the skin seems
To slough off

Flakes of mica
Disappear

For every imprint
There is a negative

For every forgotten flower

Quietly closeted / somewhere
For every hand there is another

In the cloudy folds
Of the brain

Everything we have ever known

Is only waiting for its opposite
Its other half to leap

Into the positive light

Clapped in its bronze arms
And swinging

Back and forth like bells
Endlessly touching each other / out loud

The almost invisible / the one
Smallest fraction grows

Into the giant watermelon of the tongue
Banging back and forth / and spurting

Foaming / fizzing / cascading
The brilliant amber of its voice beating

Into the open marigold of a body

That stays in one place / leaving
Only to return again

In such gallant continuity
The high ancient paean
Of the bell towers of mankind

The huge metal sails vibrate
Like a hive of singing bees

The liquid notes peal
Every hour on the hour

The sweet, steadfast cells of love
Forever replacing each other / and ringing.

VI. Though We Live Between Jaws

Dear X,

If we're beautiful as a bell dropped,
clasping each other close, contented
at the bottom of the well of sky,

If in the midst of pestilence, famine, war,
even in the midst of death if the great world
harp strings us up to new heights
clanging like crystal, like mountain peaks

Also in our greatest joys, sweetest
mornings together it intrudes,
flaming like a wall of terrible roses

So that I weep, I cannot contain myself
in the black midnight wood
listening to the cicadas on their stilts pray
on their knees above us like tall angels,

Hearing the bray of the cock for love
brassiest at dawn but always, afterwards
the dull dying away fall of his song,

With fire in the nostrils,
tongue like a wooden clapper I cry out
Mind, be quiet. Mouth, be still.
There's blood up to the blue ceiling.

Heart Attack

I do not think I do not think.

The storm labors the city,
Belabors. Battles.
Blows upon it, groaning
Like a huge ship
At sea with·no berth.

Last night on the telephone you said
"Silent heart attack."
Yes. Yours.

But mine too, and nothing's
To think but to do, do
The words come
Cawing like black crows

Face the cardiogram
Calmly, with no fuss
Eat light, sleep late

So I say, and do
Rejoice for the rest of the sweet
Life that's left to us, and keep

Smiling,
Even when you rise from bed
Only to go to the bathroom I hide,
I make my reassuring smile,

I do not think
That this tic in my eyelid, this twitch,
This ticker in the old I, redbird
Of the frightened blood beating

This storm of terror's anything
But temporary I do not think I do not think
I have no home but yours.

The World Pressing Itself Upon Us

Slipping out of the sleeping bag of our love
Only for a little, to try it
In the warm bedroom, in the city

I am astonished, at first
The air is so empty, I am naked
None of your arms enfold me

Nevertheless I must walk
Once in awhile by myself,

Delicately / delicately step
Among the immensities remembering—

Canoes in frozen rapids. Vomit.
Upset. The froth of overturn. Gear
Below zero wet. Dripping. That night

Long ago in Alaska
The two lovers, the friends
Huddled together for life—

Puddles of clothes are drifting
Like icebergs across the floor.

But even in broad daylight, despatched
About my ordinary business

It is so strange / without you

Dressed only in my thin skin I shiver
Ragged as the long howl of a wolf

And though I belong to you only
And would remain with you forever

It is for each of us, alone
Out there in all those Arctic deserts
Teeth flying like snow

Always to step carefully, to remember
With or without each other the question,
Under the stars the meaning

The world pressing itself upon us
As if we belonged to it, out there
Eternity hovering / like ice.

Summer Solstice

(6/21/81)

All morning on the screen porch
I have been trying to live up to it.

Soon the weight of it will begin,
The drag of water against walking

But just barely:

Fifty years' breathing seem to have blown away
Like pieces of milkweed, tiny stars receding

In a soft, unnameable drift
Of gray fuzz.

Are the days getting longer
Without me?

I know there are traps ahead

But I am too light headed to care,
Too absent to be brought down.

Years ago, when you came,
You lifted me out of a dark growling,

You tore me out of winter
Almost entirely.

Now, seated among the loose nets of the trees
Up here on my porch

A cold gust rattles the frames.

I know there are storms coming:
The fabric is starting to rip.

I know there are starved bellies
And armies of chaos out there, and eyes

Crying out to be filled,

But this is my world to walk in
Too:

For a little while, dissolved in it,
You and the wind hold my hand.

How fortunate I have been!

Far ahead of me the trembling
Transparent green galaxies of the leaves.

Dust City

Where we are kissing each other
in a city of telephone poles

where we are kissing each other

in a metal city
a city of electrical plants
and chemical waste paper factories

where we are kissing each other
in a city of dry industrial stink

where it is warm and wet
the round bone of your body
resting on the smooth one of mine

where we are kissing each other
on the mattress of the iron bed

there is a river of dust
there is a live forest
full of enormous frogs and pearls

Something About Sticks

Something about cold streams
in winter,

something about sticks snagged
under a thin skin of ice.

One twig like a foot
drags downstream:

in the low, gurgling choke
and rattle of pebble against pebble

I have always heard our voices.

Tangled like bare branches
your legs angle over mine:

splintered kindling, in a heap
my fingers splay across your chest

wet leaves, barbed wire
lashed around itself

in a world no one ever visits

because it's too far from town
and too high, somewhere beyond time

in these cold slices
of white ice, transparent

you'd have to look close

even to notice us,
stiff arms and legs braced

under the rind of winter

in the bend of an elbow steadfast
in black water.

In the Middle of the Worst Sickness

In the middle of the worst sickness yet
Most of the time you slept.

Flung on the bed like a loose skein of yarn

You were as patient as an old dog stretched out
On the back seat of a car in a parking lot.

No books. No TV. Occasionally I'd read to you,
But very little: perhaps we'd mention friends

Or hold hands, as if we'd never quarreled.

With starched nurses for fence posts,
With intravenous tubes for lifelines,

Slow, slow, the pale serum dropped
Infinitesimally from above.

They told us you were getting better,
But three times, in the night

Gray-faced, your teeth yellowed and clacked.

Shaking the bed, delirious
You clutched the hot water bottle till it burned you.

Even so, even so.

The more terror banged at the door
The more we clung to each other.

Outside I suppose things went on
As usual: I was too worried to notice.

Chewing my fingers, making lists

How to Get an Ambulance,
Airplane Tickets, How Much...

Inside, after the nurses left
We'd ask each other, "Was that right?"

I was always rushing to the main desk to check
And then hurrying back to you, to rest.

For if we were planted in that room we were growing.

Breathing in and out
Quietly, quietly,

Even in the midst of it we knew
What else was there to do?

Exhausted, with the stunned faces
Of gaunt Indian cattle we browsed

Over the bare fields of earth.

The smooth walls reflected
A kind of gray, feathery light,

But entering the calm lake of that room
On tiptoe, careful not to disturb you,

Always the lurching gyroscope of my life tilted
And then settled,

Swaying slightly, with your breath

At the center of the world we lay peacefully
As birds in a nest

For the odd thing about it is that often there is no noise
Or practically none, at the scene of the accident

The town fire alarm just stops

And the victims are speechless,
Having done everything they could,

The crowd stands around waiting,

In deep grass cows stare
At the overturned car, still quivering,

After the roar of sirens, the fume
And boil of anxiety we emerge

Into this soundlessness as if it were a small glider

Where we sit motionless, in our ears
Only the soft sough of air,

Only a confused gratefulness in our heads
Like overgrown chrysanthemums to be pruned,

Once more cut down, snipped off,
All that is unnecessary thrown away

Into this white silence like the silence
Of incubators, the wrinkled flesh of birth,

Here in this room where we are both held
In some incredible suspension

Cloud-soft, beyond time drifting
On the lap of earth.

Over Our Dead Bodies

1

Your arm

Lies on my lap like a live log
Steaming mahogany, a mitten

Five roasted chestnuts
Suddenly bursting into blossom

The blaze shoots up my shoulder
And through my rib cage

Like a warm day, a wool blanket
That will never end

2

Even though the town reservoir
Turns into a mill race
Roaring downhill

And sweeping us before it
In the icy current gasping

Struggling to keep our heads up
In a few seconds we will drown

We will shoot over the sluiceways
Like waterlogged canoes,

Livid bellies churning,
Choking black stones

Your arm will reach out
Over our dead bodies I swear
We will reach dry land together

3

For our clasped hands
Are bedded down here

In the clay pots of our marriage
Like two zinnias, two bachelor buttons
Side by side, dreaming

Whole conflagrations of villages,
The smell of cloves like incense

Sprinkling its red petals through the air
In the furnace of the true fire

That will fuse everything into clear glass,
One transparent globe

With the sky resting in it like sapphire.

Though We Live between Jaws

And even though we live between jaws
Precarious, perched in the branches of trees,

Though we stagger from storm to storm

Though the eye at the center is an empty lighthouse
Scanning the blank waves,

Though the houses of our lives are holes
Scooped out of the air,

Still I would have us live here forever,
Breathing into each other's mouths

Like blown eggshells teetering
Like birdsnests, from side to side,

Though the houses of our lives are nothing

But soft puffballs, as permanent
As summer clouds, as secure

As the sudden sucking gulp of a swimmer
At the last gasp, the pink

Blossom of the failing lungs

Though all the beloved hands, eyes,
White foreheads, hair

All profiles of the moon
Like ancient sailing vessels shipwreck

In the shivering wrath of the ocean,
In the high gyroscope of the hurricane

Over the horizon who knows

Along the deserted miles of beach
What startled child's voice

Sharp as a seagull's cry may lift

Years later, at one of our gloves,
A handkerchief puffed up like a peony

In the froth at the edge of the shore floating
Till even the gold circle

Of the ring we make out of nothingness

May breathe once more, in the pocket
Of two crystals, in the bright

Brief world of the wave breaking.

After the First Embrace

We are separated   almost at once
    From every airport we are calling

As the wash of liquid heat
    Disperses itself   love

Thins out, cooling
    Over the whole globe,

But after the first embrace
    In Sacramento there will be one pocket,
        Here and there others,

A few cooking fires   friends
    That still remain to us   flickering
        Just over the lip of earth,

Gathered around the hearth signalling
    Greetings from nowhere
        Touchable...

As the messages come back, jittering
    Over the torn wires

Lying in bed, we listen
    To the tapes they send, spoken

Days past, the children
    Fly back and forth, believers

They grow tomatoes, bread
    Rises   in small ovens,

Thread knots itself into islands
    Clusters of people waving

For the lacework of our lives
    Is so fragile, by day

From East to West fingertips
    Ravel, reach for each other...

But talking all night like candles
    In the windows of the young

Though we gutter out by morning
    In Mexico, China, Greece,
        Each face cannot be present

Every minute   where are you
    Though the fabric rots   the pain

Holds us together   here
    In Cuba, Alaska, New Zealand

Fire shoots across the heavens
    Or falls in the water, stunned

Tongues speak, burning
    Chunks of meteorites whose absence

Is not absence   in this life waking
    In darkness   we hear each other's voices

We who are one body
    We who are one body.

Books of Poetry by Patricia Goedicke

The Wind of Our Going, Copper Canyon Press, 1985
The King of Childhood, Confluence Press, 1984
Crossing the Same River, University of Massachusetts Press, 1980
The Dog That Was Barking Yesterday, Lynx House, 1980
The Trail That Turns on Itself, Ithaca House, 1978
For the Four Corners, Ithaca House, 1976
Between Oceans, Harcourt, Brace & World, Inc., 1968

Both Patricia Goedicke and her husband, Leonard Wallace Robinson, are writers; he a former *New Yorker* writer as well as a novelist, short story writer, and poet; she a poet who has published seven earlier books of poetry. Both are New Englanders, but lived and wrote in Mexico for many years before they moved to Missoula, Montana, where Goedicke now teaches in the Creative Writing Program of the University of Montana.